WHEN YOU
Fast

© Copyright 2018 by Crystal Wilson

This document is geared towards providing exact and reliable information in regards to the topic and issue covered. The publication is sold with the idea that the publisher is not required to render accounting, officially permitted, or otherwise, qualified services. If advice is necessary, legal or professional, a practiced individual in the profession should be ordered.

From a Declaration of Principles which was accepted and approved equally by a Committee of the American Bar Association and a Committee of Publishers and Associations.

In no way is it legal to reproduce, duplicate, or transmit any part of this document in either electronic means or in printed format. Recording of this publication is strictly prohibited and any storage of this document is not allowed unless with written permission from the publisher. All rights reserved.

The information provided herein is stated to be truthful and consistent, in that any liability, in terms of inattention or otherwise, by any usage or abuse of any policies, processes, or directions contained within is the solitary and utter responsibility of the recipient reader. Under no circumstances will any legal responsibility or blame be held against the publisher for any reparation, damages, or monetary loss due to the information herein, either directly or indirectly.

Respective authors own all copyrights not held by the publisher.

The information herein is offered for informational purposes solely, and is universal as so. The presentation of the information is without contract or any type of guarantee assurance.

The trademarks that are used are without any consent, and the publication of the trademark is without permission or backing by the trademark owner. All trademarks and brands within this book are for clarifying purposes only and are the owned by the owners themselves, not affiliated with this document.

All Scripture quotation, unless otherwise indicated, are taken from the Holy Bible, New International Version®. NIV®. Copyright © 1973, 1978, 1984 by International Bible Society. Used by permission of Zondervan Publishing House. All rights reserved.

ISBN: 978-1-943409-50-1

All Rights Reserved

WHEN YOU
FAST

DISCOVER THE UNTOLD TRUTH ABOUT FASTING

Crystal Wilson

www.PureThoughtsPublishing.com
Conyers, GA

Dedication

I WOULD LIKE TO dedicate this book to my family.

I love you Mom, you are a God fearing women and because of you I am becoming a Proverbs 31 women. I thank you mom for training me up in the Lord at a young age and keeping me and Shannon in Church. Because of you, I have truly learned the meaning of Proverbs 22:6. Although I strayed away from God at one point and time in my life. I always had the word inside of me and I thank you and Dad for that.

Dad, I thank you for raising me up to be a go getter, to be independent and for teaching me that everything in life I can have as long as I work hard for it.

Shannon, my dear and loving sister. I love you so much sis and I am so happy that our relationship has grown the way it has. I thank God for you and how much you appreciate the woman of God that I strive to be. I thank you for your positivity, your love and your support in my endeavors to pursue my dreams.

To my husband, Tony I am so grateful to have you as my husband and I thank God for bringing us together. We have been through so much throughout the years and I thank you for sticking by me through thick and thin. I am enjoying watching you become a Man of God. I love you

To my Children, Antoine, Catherine & Andrew. I thank God for giving me charge over your lives and I can't wait to see you walk in the purpose that God has planned for your life. I pray that this book will bless you.

To my Mother-in-Law, Aileen Reed. I thank God for you as well. I am so blessed to have you as a Mother in law, I thank you for your love and support in me and Tony's time of need. I pray that God gives you all of your hearts desires.

To my Father-in-Law, Eugene Wilson. I love the relationship that we have and I thank God for using me as a vessel to you. You have been so loving, kind and supportive and I really appreciate that.

Acknowledgements

I FIRST HAVE TO give honor to my savior, my redeemer! I thank God for giving me the vision to write this book. It was only through your grace and mercy that I was able to complete this task. I thank you God for downloading each and every word, scripture, revelation and impartation for "When you Fast".

I have to honor those who came before me with a powerful anointing. Pastor Jentezen Franklin, Bishop TD Jakes & Dr. Myles Monroe. I have to acknowledge them because their teachings inspired me while I was in the process of writing this devotional; I thank God for their influences that helped me to come up with my own tools and strategies for "When You Fast."

I also have to acknowledge the deceased Reverend Roscoe C. Wilson Sr. of my home church, Saint John Baptist church. I thank you for baptizing me in the Name of Jesus with the Father, Son and the Holy Spirit. I was nine years old when I was baptized and little did I know this is when my journey began.

I would like to thank my friend, my sister in Christ Latoya Rivers. I thank God for you and I know that our relationship was a divine connection. I met you at a time in my life where I was going through a transition. I thank you for being my prayer warrior and my mentor. I thank God for using you in my life. I love you.

Last but not least, I would like to acknowledge Pure Thoughts Publishing LLC. And their team (Marita Kinney, Varun KC, Samantha Edgerton, Donato Toledo and Milos J.). You all helped me to finally put this masterpiece together and I love you all for that, I thank God for you!

What will this inspirational devotional help you achieve?

- Draw Nearer to God
- Increase your prayer & worship lifestyle
- With God's help reach your fitness goals quickly.
- Learn to be more disciplined towards food choices
- Experience a spiritual breakthrough
- Becoming more spiritually aware of God's presence
- Gain true spiritual Health and Wellness

Prayers

The Sinners Prayer (Psalm 51)

THE SINNERS PRAYER IS a consecration prayer and is for those who want to renew their relationship with Jesus Christ. For those of you that are reading this for the first time, and you heard that voice inside of you say "pick up that book", read this prayer out loud:

> Prayer:
>
> Dear Lord God, I am a sinner, and I need you in my life. I ask for forgiveness for all of the wrong things that I have done. I thank you for dying on the cross for me, and I believe you were resurrected. I am so sick and tired of doing things my way. I invite you to rule over my life as Savior and king. Fill me with you Holy Spirit, wash me and make me brand new. Help me to grow a newfound love for you as my father. Help me to trust you every day and in every area of my life. Help me to live for you and only you. In Jesus Name Amen.

The Repentance prayer (Matthew 4:17)

Repentance is defined as telling God that you are sorry for something wrong that you have done. Repentance allows you to turn away from what you are doing wrong and turn to Jesus Christ. For those of you that may be reading this book for the first time, and you don't know Jesus, but want to get to know him, say the following prayer below

Prayer:

Dear Lord God, you know my heart from the inside and out. There is nothing that I can hide from you. Father God I ask that you purify me, wash me clean and allow me to receive true salvation today from your son Jesus Christ. Dear father, I urge you to show me what is unpleasing to you about my life. (Pause for about one minute…whatever comes to your mind, ask God to forgive you for that very thing). I receive Christ in my life today; I am being made new, Hallelujah, in Jesus name Amen!

Step One

Prepare yourself spiritually:

*Go before God and tell him that you want to fast, next establish what you want to fast for? (a new job, a promotion, weight-loss goals, a new career path, a rebellious child, a family member that may be dealing with an addiction, you marriage, health or a financial or spiritual breakthrough etc.). This is because you want to establish what you are fasting for, you want the fast to not only change your life but to be worth it to you and God).

*Next, ask the Holy Spirit to lead you to what type of fast you will do

Different Types of Fast:

Intermittent Fast—No food or water...you ask how long? However, God leads you.

This type of fast is not letting anybody know, demons that are listening or watching you don't get a chance to try and stop you.

(When someone dies, and you are going through a spiritual change when you are fighting inner demons with yourself or someone,

Liquid Fast—Liquid Fasting puts YOU back in control of your life (water, juice)

Three day fast—give up at least one item of food

Partial Fast—6: am-12 noon, 12 noon to 6: oo pm, 6:00 am-3 pm, 6:00 am-6:00 pm, or 6:00 pm to 6:00 am.

You have to ask yourself, what are you willing to give up to reach your spiritual or fitness goals?

Step Two

Prepare yourself prior:

TWO WEEKS PRIOR YOU want to rid yourself of caffeine, chocolate, sweet candies, sweet juice, bread, and starches. If your body is used to having these foods daily, then you are going to have a rough time. Try to prepare yourself so that you won't experience nauseous, headaches and weakness.

Step Three

(Apply the Word to help you along the way)

*AFTER YOU HAVE ESTABLISHED what type of fast you will do, with the help of the holy spirit apply the scriptures to help you with you fast (Matthew 6:16-18, Matthew 9: 15-15, Luke 18:9-14, Mark 2:18-22, Luke 5:33-39, Daniel 9:3, I will go over these in more detail). The devil is going to attack, expect it, he doesn't want you to get your breakthrough so be prepared (Matthew 4:1-11)

*Apply scriptures according to your situation (finances, marriage) you want to speak life as you are fasting

Step Four

(WATCH GOD'S MANIFESTATION, NOT just throughout the fast but long after).

Scriptures about Fasting

"MOREOVER WHEN YE FAST, be not as the hypocrites, of a sad countenance: for they disfigure their faces that they may appear unto men to fast. Verily I say unto you; they have their reward. But thou, when you fast, anoint thine head and wash thy face, that thou appear not unto men to fast, but unto thy Father Which is in secret: and thy Father, which seethe in secret, shall reward thee openly."

Matthew 6:16-18

(This passage talks about not broadcasting your fasting, although you may be going through a serious change, try to keep fasting between you and God, unless doing corporate fasting, try not to look so drained and stay refreshed, if you feel weak, gain your strength from God).

> "Then came to him the disciples of John, saying, why do we, and the Pharisees fast oft, but thy disciples fast not? And Jesus said unto them, Can the children of the bride chamber mourn, as long as the bridegroom is with them? But days will come when the bridegroom shall be taken from them, and then shall they fast."
>
> *Matthew 9: 14-15*

(Jesus is saying to the Pharisee, why would the disciples have to fast when I am right here in the Physical walking and talking with them daily? Jesus had so much wisdom. He knew there would be a time when he no longer would be here with us in the Physical but in the Spiritual and that would be the time to fast, that time would be now!)

To some who were confident of their own righteousness and looked down on everyone else, Jesus told this parable: "Two men went up to the temple to pray, one a Pharisee and the other a tax collector. The Pharisee stood by himself and prayed: 'God, I thank you that I am not like other people-robbers, evildoers, and adulterers-or even like this tax collector. I fast twice a week and give a tenth of all I get.' "But the tax collector stood at a distance. He would not even look up to heaven, but beat his breast and said, 'God, have mercy on me, a sinner.' "I tell you that this man, rather than the other, went home justified before God. For all those who exalt they will be humbled, and those who humble themselves will be exalted."

Luke 18:9-14

(Sometimes we think more highly of ourselves than we should. When you get ready to fast God is going to show you your true self.)

Now John's disciples and the Pharisees were fasting. Some people came and asked Jesus, "How is it that John's disciples and the disciples of the Pharisees are fasting, but yours are not?" [19] Jesus answered, "How can the guests of the bridegroom fast while he is with them? They cannot, so long as they have him with them. [20] But the time will come when the bridegroom will be taken from them, and on that day they will fast. [21]" No one sews a patch of unshrunk cloth on an old garment. Otherwise, the new piece will pull away from the old, making the tear worse. [22] And no one pours new wine into old wineskins. Otherwise, the wine will burst the skins, and both the wine and the wineskins will be ruined. No, they pour new wine into new wineskins."

Mark 2:18-22

(The Pharisees were jealous of the disciples; they were what you called "haters". They questioned Jesus about why they had to fast, but the disciples didn't. Jesus was known as the bridegroom, and Jesus told the Pharisees that the reason why the disciples weren't fasting is that they were walking with Him daily. Jesus was wise and said that there would be a time where he would be no longer with them physically but spiritually. That is the time when the disciples would fast.

So I turned to the Lord God and pleaded with him in prayer and petition, in fasting, and in sackcloth and ashes.

Daniel 9:3

(This is your time to cry out God! Be real with him and tell him all of your issues and problems. Make all of you request known to him and watch God transform your life throughout the next 21 chapters.)

Healthy Foods for Fasting

- No fried foods
- Baked Chicken, Fish, Salmon, Tuna, Shrimp
- All fruits are allowed
- All beans are permitted
- plenty of green vegetables- collard greens, green beans, peas, broccoli, cabbage, mustard greens, kale, spinach, asparagus, romaine lettuce, cucumbers
- all other vegetables- potatoes, sweet potatoes, corn, carrots, beets, tomatoes
- Nuts and berries (walnuts, peanuts, almonds, cashews, cranberries, raisins,
- No dairy products (no milk or cheese)
- ONLY WATER (no sodas or fruit juices)

Foods to eat when breaking a fast:

*Raw fruits and vegetables (Watermelon, strawberries, lettuce, spinach, kale)

Soup

Tips:

- If you are fasting from meat, be very careful about introducing it back into your diet when the fast is complete. Start off with Tuna or soup (due to sickness or stomach pains).
- You also want to make sure that you are spending some quality time with God, remember you are also doing this for you! Make sure to worship, listen to inspirational music or inspirational sermons, pray on your own about things that you want God to do in your life (James4:2-3)
- **FASTING WILL DESTROY HEADACHES!!! EVERYTHING THAT WAS CAUSING YOU STRESS WILL COME OUT OF YOUR BODY.**
- Watch God Manifest quickly in your life; God loves the fact that you are seeking him through prayer and fasting so if you fall off, don't get discouraged, we are in this together!

Contents

Surrendering to God...29
The Benefits of Your Worship..33
One Day at a time 37
The Armor of God 41
Spiritual Warfare & Demonic Attacks....................................45
Discipline 49
Completion..53
Revelation...57
The Spirit of Addiction...61
The Prayer Closet..65
The Halfway Mark..69
Discipleship 73
A Lifestyle of Fasting 77
Health & Wellness 81
The Detoxing Process 85
Spiritual Gifts (The Holy Spirit)..89
Generational Curses 95
Faith 99
The Anointing 105
Favor...109
Breakthrough...113

Day 1

Surrendering to God

Therefore I urge you, brethren, by the mercies of God, to present your bodies a living and holy sacrifice, acceptable to God, which is your spiritual service of worship.

(Romans 12:1)

- The definition of surrender is to submit to power or control of another (which of course is Jesus Christ). Today release all of your issues and stress to God...by doing this, you are giving God Total control over your life. Ask God to take over your Mind, body and soul, subjecting your thoughts to him *(2 Corinthians 10:5)*. When you give God total control, you will feel a release, your worries will start to go away, and God will give you so much peace *(Philippians 4:7)*. I know this is hard to do, but this is giving God total control over your situation, not knowing what the outcome will be.

CONTINUE TO SEEK GOD throughout the day and ask him to lead you into what food/s you need to give up. This isn't going to be easy but remember; we are in this together. Remember to drink plenty of water throughout the day. If you feel the need to grab something unhealthy, or feel as if you want to back out of the fast go to God (either in prayer or by the reading of his word), remember we are weak, but Jesus Christ makes us strong! *But he said to me, "My grace is sufficient for you, for my power is made perfect in weakness." Therefore I will boast all the more gladly about my weaknesses, so that Christ's power may rest on me. 10 That is why, for Christ's sake, I delight in weaknesses, in insults, in hardships, in persecutions, in difficulties. For when I am weak, then I am strong. (2 Corinthians 12:9-11). Release all of your issues and problems to God today!* Also keep in mind, the enemy hates the fact that you are surrending to God so be prepared for attacks to come in many different ways and forms (an employee or employer bringing donuts or sweets to your job, a family member offering you something that you know you shouldn't eat or even for those married, the devil may use your spouse to try and discourage you from fasting. The enemy will try to use these tactics to get you to fall off but be strong and know that you will be tested! Remember, Jesus was tested also when he fasted (*Matthew 4:1-11*)

Prayer

Father God in Jesus Name we come before you right now at this hour first thanking you for this day. Lord, we ask that you forgive us for our sins and we repent right now (this is the time to repent of all your wrong doing before surrendering, anything that comes to your mind ask God to forgive you for it). Lord, we also pray that you show us who we need to forgive at this time (anyone that comes into your mind that you need to forgive, do it, if you need to go back and make it right with this person, do it!, you don't want the spirit of unforgivness to hinder your blessing/s (Mark 11:25). Father God, show us what we need to surrender to you today (food, money, children, marriage, stress, health issues, addiction, etc.). Knowing that you told us in your word to cast all of our cares before you, Lord we give you all difficult issues in our lives right now and leave them with you (1 Peter 5:7). Lord we ask for your strength right now in Jesus name, knowing that we can't do this alone, we need your help to guide us along the way. We come against every stronghold and tactics that Satan and his demons will try to use to prevent us from gaining our spiritual breakthrough. We put all of our hope and trust in you and thank you for the blessings you have given us. In Jesus name, we pray, Amen!

Questions/Reflection

1. What are you going to give up for 21 days?
2. What has God revealed to you today?
3. What or who are you being led to pray for today?

Day 2

The Benefits of Your Worship

Let everything that has breath praise the Lord. Praise the Lord.

(Psalm 150:6)

- *The definition of Worshiping is to show reverence and adoration for

WORSHIP IS GOING TO play a huge part in this as well as helping your Sprit Man get through the next 21 days. You can worship God in many different ways (For Example: Praise him, lift your hands, shout hallelujah, sing to him, tell him Thank you for all he has done in your life and all that he has blessed you with, (speaking in your heavenly language, we will discuss this is a later chapter). Try to get in the habit of having a heart to worship whenever necessary. Worship has so many benefits, not only does it relieve you from stress and worry but it also invites the presence of the Holy Spirit around you. It is a feeling like no other once the Holy Spirit comes upon you. (Acts 2:1-13). Try to start worshiping for 5 min, then 10, then 20 until it increases. At first, it may seem hard, and you may feel as though you are having to push yourself to worship (this is because you are having a battle between your flesh man vs.

spirit man). The Longer you worship, the deeper the presence of God gets, and you will lose yourself in the presence of God and also lose track of time. The more you worship, the more God will reveal things to you. God can also give you visions and dreams if you happen to worship and then fall asleep (I discovered this from my personal experience). God will also show you people you need to pray for, things concerning your overall life, things concerning your business and spiritual attacks that may be coming for you and your family. I have also noticed with my personal experience that worship becomes more intense when you are fasting because you are breaking down your flesh man and building up your spirit. Try to set some time aside to worship today, and I promise you will have an encounter with God that you will never forget!

Prayer

Father God in the Name of Jesus, I come before you right now with a heart to worship. Lord, help me to find time out of my day (morning, noon or evening) to worship you. Father God help me to learn to worship you in Spirit and in Truth and whenever I am led to (John 4:24). Help me to learn to worship you in many different ways, In Jesus Name I pray Amen!

Questions/Reflection

1. In what ways will you or have you're found to Worship God today?
2. How do you think Worship will benefit your life?
3. How did/do you feel after your Worship?

Day 3

One Day at a time

"Therefore, do not worry about tomorrow, for tomorrow will worry about itself. Each Day has enough trouble of its own."

Matthew 6:34

CONGRATULATIONS, YOU HAVE MADE it to Day Three...you should be very proud of yourself, and the fact that you have made is this far. Don't forget that God is honoring your sacrifice so don't get discouraged (Psalm 50:23). If you consume caffeine, starches and sweets before the fast, you may be dealing with headaches and nausea. Don't worry I have experienced this too in the past. This is the process of your body detoxing and riding itself of toxins. Just make sure that you consume plenty of water. You may also be having a lot of gas; this is because your stomach is being cleansed. This is the Day where you must command your flesh to be subject to your spirit. If you are doing a liquid or intermittent fast, every time you get hunger pains go to God in prayer. He will help you get through this! Building up your spirit man is very important and will help you discipline your body (which we will discuss on Day 6).

Prayer

Father God in the Name of Jesus, we need your strength, grace, and mercy to get us through this. We can't and won't do this without you. Lord when our flesh is fighting against us, help us to turn to you at all times by praying, worshiping, reading your word and reaching out to group members and loved ones that can encourage us. As you said in your word, the Spirit is willing, but our flesh is weak (Matthew 26:14). Help us to understand that through fasting we will learn with the help of the Holy Spirit to command our flesh to be subject to your spirit. We know that this won't be an easy task, so we pray for consistency and persistence, In Jesus Name Amen!

Questions/Reflection

1. How are you feeling today?
2. What Foods or drinks have you been struggling to give up thus far?
3. Write down some things that you need the Holy Spirit to help you with

Day 4

The Armor of God

"Finally, my brethren be strong in the Lord, and in the power of his might. Put on the whole armor of God, that ye may able to stand against the wiles of the devil."

Ephesians 6:10-11

PUTTING ON THE FULL "Armor of God" is very important because this is your defense strategy against the enemy. This strategy has also helped me to fight a lot of my Spiritual battles. The Armor of God is God's clothing and (for anyone in the military, "full battle rattle"). Think of how a soldier is dressed before he goes to war. He has his helmet/ caviler, breastplate, belt, sword/gun, shield, and shoes. When you wake up the first thing you should do is put on the "Helmet of Salvation". This is going to protect your mind (any thought trying to come into your mind or go out). The Second, "The Breastplate of Righteousness," this means that your heart should be open to forgiveness and you are not easily offended. It also means to have a heart of repentance, so that you can be covered by the grace of God. If not, we leave ourselves open to Satan, and he will use unforgiveness against us. Thirdly, "The Belt of Truth", Allow God's truth to surround you like a belt, try to be truthful in everything that you do. Fourth, "The Sword of the Spirit" this means that you are ready for action! You must know the truth (which is the Word of God) so that when the enemy comes with his lies, you won't fall into his deceptive ways (read Ephesians 6: 10:18).

Prayer

Father God in the Name of Jesus, we come before you to put on your full Armor so that we can stand against the wiles of the devil. We put on the Helmet of Salvation right now in the Name of Jesus. Lord protect our mind right now & allow us to stay focused on you throughout our day. We cast down every thought that is not like you in Jesus Name. We put on the breastplate of righteousness; help us not to be easily offended on today. Help us to take the negative things that people say to us with a grain of salt. Lord, we also ask right now that you forgive us of all of our sins, help us to have the heart to repent to you on a daily basis, no matter how big or small the sin is. Also, help us to go back and make it right with anyone that we have not forgiven (so that no unforgiveness will harbor in our hearts. Dear Jesus, help us to walk in the Belt of Truth on Today, allowing the truth of your word to surround us like a belt. Allow us to not only be truthful to you but to our spouse, children, friends and family every day. Lastly, allow us to take up the Sword of the Spirt, which is our weapon. Help us to remember your Word in the time of need (which is whenever the enemy is trying to deceive us, or trick us with his tactics). In Jesus Name I pray, Amen.

Questions/Reflection

1. How will putting on the Armor of God change your life on a daily basis?
2. Imagine dressing with the Armor of God when you wake up in the morning (just like you but on your regular clothes).
3. Spiritually Put on the Armor of God daily before you go to work, school, or into an important business meeting and watch God fight on your behalf!

Day 5

Spiritual Warfare & Demonic Attacks

"For we wrestle not against flesh and blood, but against principalities, against powers, against the rulers of darkness of this world, against spiritual wickedness in high places.

Ephesians: 6-12

I WILL NEVER FORGET the attack that I experience one night after I prayed for my Sister, my stepson's mother and my Father. I remember having a dream that felt so real like Satan himself was trying to attack me. I literally saw a vision on my wall of a demonic figure with horns on top of its head, coming to me with a knife. I remember trying to yell out Jesus in my sleep, but it was almost like my mouth and body were bound; I couldn't speak. I tried my best to yell out Jesus' name (which was very hard), and when I did, the dream stopped. I never in my life experienced something like this, and at that very moment, I knew it was time to start digging deeper into my prayer life and the Word of God, the Devil was not playing with me. Spiritual Warfare is real and so are Demonic Attacks, and you should expect them a lot more while you are fasting. Why?

because the enemy is threatened by your sacrifice to God and he knows that you are closer to your breakthrough than you could ever imagine. We also have to remember that we are in a constant spiritual battle and the enemy is going to try and make you feel defeated by bringing stress, fear, doubt and worry. Spiritual Warfare has many forms. For example: trying to read your bible and you keep falling asleep, struggling with praying or finding time to pray, Praying and being interrupted by a crying child or a phone call or struggling to get up early in the morning and pray. In any shape or form you feel as if you are in a constant struggle with your flesh to read God's word and pray, my friend this is a form of Spiritual Warfare. Demonic Attacks can come in many different forms also. For example: A child having a scary dream, having experience with the "hag" riding your back (when you sense an evil presence in the room, you fall asleep and feel a heavy weight on your chest- almost like you are bound and cannot move or speak) or having a spirit of fear. Demonic attacks can also come in the form of someone you care about (a rebellious child, arguing with your spouse or another family member or co-workers coming against you). These are all forms of attacks because we have to remember that we are not wrestling against flesh and blood but against a spirit. We also have to keep in mind that the Enemy is going to try and use the people that are closest to you (which are more than likely your children, family members or a spouse, 1 Peter 5:8-9). Although these attacks will come because this is Satan's job, the best thing that the people of God can do is to put on the full Armor of God and stay Prayed up!

Prayer

God Our Father in Jesus Name, we come before you this day to thank you for getting us to the 5th day of the 21 day Fast. Lord, we want to thank you for the blessings that you have given us thus far. Lord, we ask this day that you help us to recognize when Spiritual or Demonic Attacks are trying to make it to our household. Lord, help us to have discernment when spiritual or Demonic attacks may be coming our way. As you said in your word 1 Peter 5:89, help us to be sober and vigilant at all times so that we can stand firm on your word. Help us to speak the Word of God against the enemy so that we can stand against the wiles of the devil, in Jesus name Amen!

Questions/Reflection

1. Have you encountered any Spiritual attacks in the past? If you did, what did you do about it?
2. Do you feel as if you could recognize a Spiritual or Demonic attack?

Day 6

Discipline

"But I keep under my body, and bring it into subjection: lest that by any means when I have preached to others, I should be a cast-away."

1 Corinthians 9:27

TO LEARN DISCIPLINE IN any area of your life whether is with worship, prayer, exercise or food it is going to take time. It is not easy at first and takes much dedication and practice. I want to discuss some steps with you to help you gain discipline. I would also like to share some of my constant struggles. You must establish that you can do nothing without God's help (I have had my experience with this, and when I have tried to do it my way, I have failed). You also have to understand that you may be the only one in your house fasting or willing to fast. God may use you to get your family to eat healthier or gain a lifestyle of fasting but remember, you need God to help you show your spouse/children this. This is one of my constant struggles, and sometimes I feel as though I am the only spiritual and faith-based individual in my household. I also feel as though sometimes I am the only one in my home that is trying to maintain a healthy lifestyle. This is why it is important to work and prepare your meals before beginning your fast. By doing this, you won't be tempted to eat sweets or fried foods. I find when I often prep my meals and freeze them, it helps me stay determined. You may also end up having to cook separate meals while fasting. For example, if you are only eating vegetables and fruits more than likely, your family is probably going to want to eat meat for the next 21 days. This can be very hard and frustrating at times, but know that with God's help you are not alone (John 15:4-5). You must push yourself with the help of the Holy Spirit. Ask yourself this next question, how bad do I want to_____(Get delivered, get saved, maintain a healthy lifestyle, gain discipline when it comes to food, protect my family, spouse or children from addiction, get closer to God, gain spiritual well-being, get more revelation, etc.). Whatever your reason is, this is going to help you increase your discipline, so stay focused on why you decided to fast in the first place (proverbs 4:25).

Prayer

Holy Spirit, we need your help today. Help us to establish ways that will help us to remain disciplined towards this fast. Father, we need you to help us gain a lifestyle of discipline. We also need you to grant us new strategies and tools to help us maintain this lifestyle of fasting. Lord, I thank you that you are honoring this fasting and we ask that you continue to lead us and guide us into an everlasting and holy experience, in Jesus Name, Amen!

Questions/Reflection

1. Ask the Holy Spirit to Show you what you need to do to learn more discipline.

Day 7

Completion

"Now, therefore, perform the doing of it; that as there was a readiness to will, so thee may be a performance also out of that which ye have."

2 Corinthians 8:11

THERE ARE MANY INSTANCES in the bible that use the number seven as a symbol. I will discuss a couple of these instances with you, for example (Genesis 1) God spends six days creating the earth and the heavens, on the 7th day He rests (which is known as the Sabbath). Exodus 22:30 also discusses animals being sacrificed after seven years of age. Last but not least, Joshua 6 talks about the battle of Jericho (in verses 3-4) the Lord tells Joshua to march around the city and get seven priests to carry seven ram horns. On the seventh day, they were to march around the city seven times. Later in verse 16, the seventh time walking around the city resulted in the Army of the Lord gaining the city! With that being said, you should be proud of yourself because you have come to a level of completion with your fast. I am positive that by now God has revealed so much to you through your discipline, dedication, and sacrifice unto him. I am also positive that many of you have experienced weight loss, pure skin, mental health, alertness and a closer relationship with God. I want to encourage you to stick with the fast; you will experience nothing but greatness from here.

Prayer

Father God in Jesus Name, I am so thankful that only you can make me complete! I thank you for allowing me to complete seven days of fasting. I know that through your grace and mercy you have brought me this far and I can only go up from here. I thank you for what you have revealed to me through your word, and I thank you for answering my prayers. Father God, help me to continue to stay disciplined so that I can experience total greatness in you. In Jesus Name I pray, Amen!

Questions/Reflection

1. How does it feel to experience this level of completion?
2. Do you feel as if you can go further with this fast?
3. What are some prayers/breakthroughs that you have experienced this far?

Day 8

Revelation

> *"That the God our Lord, Jesus Christ, the Father of glory, may give you a spirit of wisdom and of revelation in the knowledge of him."*
>
> Ephesians 1:17

BE PREPARED FOR WHAT God is going to reveal to you whether it's good or bad, ask God to prepare you for it. You want to be able to handle what is being shown to you because you may not like the outcome. Revelation is going to come in so many different ways. God is going to reveal people that you need to cut off and projects that you need to complete. You may not like or be ready for what God is going to reveal to you, but he has to do it. There may be certain friends that God may tell you to distance yourself from, not that they are bad people, but God has to work on the inside of you. For him to do that, he must get you alone in a quiet space. God has some plans that He wants you to carry out, and he needs you to be focused. I love when God reveals stuff to me because I know that he knows what's best for me (even if it hurts). You are in a season of progression, and you must be obedient in what he is telling you to do. Being disobedient in this season could very well cost you your life, your purpose and even set you back a few years. I learned this the hard way. Listen to God today, don't question that he wants you to cut that person off (even if it is a family member). Trust him and know that he will not steer you wrong.

Prayer

Father God, I thank you right now for revelation. God, I know that you know what's best for me and I thank you for giving me a spirt of discernment on today. Lord, prepare me for what you are going to show me or tell me to do. If there are people in my life that I need to distance myself from, show me right now in Jesus Name and help me to approach them about it in a loving way. Lord, I thank you for the season that I am in and ask that you give me obedience right now to carry out the plans and visons that you have placed inside of my heart. In Jesus Name I pray, Amen.

Questions/Reflection

1. Are you ready for what God is going to reveal to you?
2. What things has God revealed to you already?

Day 9

The Spirit of Addiction

"There hath no temptation taken you but such as is common to man: but God is faithful, who will not suffer you to be tempted above that ye are able, but will with the temptation also make a way to escape, that ye may be able to bear it."

1 Corinthians 10:13

THE SPIRIT OF ADDICTION is very strong and is something not a lot of people want to talk about. People can be addicted to so many different things (caffeine, sweets, chocolate, pornography, sex, food, shopping and etc.). If we can be honest with ourselves, we are all addicted to something. I want to be very transparent with you; I used to struggle with the Spirit of Masturbation. I had overcome it at one point and time in my life but, because I had strayed away from prayer and God's word for so long, I had allowed this particular demonic spirit to enter back into my life. Although it felt good to please myself, after I had done it I always felt bad and guilty. I allowed the devil to tempt me into doing it and then after I had gotten my sexual pleasure, I allowed him to condemn me. This was really serious because I began to feel bound. I always cried to God and asked him to forgive me but would end up doing it again. What I didn't realize is that God had to renew my mind and my spirt before I could overcome this demon. I feel as though God wanted me to share this with you because I wanted to be honest as to I am not perfect. The word of God says certain spirits will only come out by fasting (Matthew 17:21, Mark 9:29). This is why it is so important to develop and maintain a lifestyle of fasting. Falling back into a sin that you once got delivered from can be very hard; speaking from experience the spirit of Masturbation that I was dealing with came back even heavier and it seemed harder than before to deal with this temptation (Matthew 12:43-45). I hope that my testimony has encouraged you and that you continue to seek God through fasting and his word. Remember, you can't do this alone, you need God's help. Also, remember that God will not allow you to be tempted beyond your control and he always provides a way to escape the temptation (1 Corinthians 10:13). You are an overcomer, you've got this!

Prayer

Father God in Jesus Name, we come before you on this beautiful day thanking you for giving us the Victory over our addictions. Lord, help us not to get weary in well doing and help us not to backslide or fall back into our temptations. Lord help us to also remember 1 Corinthians 10:13, that you will not allow us to be tempted past our control and that you will always provide a way for us to escape. We ask for discernment on today on whatever that way of escape may be. Forgive us Lord for sinning over and over again. We decree and declare that we are overcomers! In Jesus Name, Amen

Questions/Reflection

1. What addictions do you feel you are struggling with on today?
2. Do you often feel defeated when you keep falling back into your addiction? Why?
3. Speak these declarations over your addiction Today (I am an overcomer, I am covered by the blood of Jesus, I have the Victory, God Gave me authority over my addiction, I am not a backslider, Jesus Loves me, Satan cannot and will not lead me into feeling condemned!)

Day 10

The Prayer Closet

"And when thou prayest, thou shalt not be as the hypocrites are: for they love to pray standing in the synagogues and the corners of the streets, that they may be seen of men. Verily I say unto you; They have their reward. But thou, when thou prayest, enter into thy closet, and when though hast shut thy door, pray to thy Father which is in secret; and thy Father which seeth in secret shall reward thee openly."

Matthew 6:5-6

Tips

PRAY GOD'S WORD BACK to him. 1.) Come to him in the Name of Jesus 2.) repent of all unforgiveness, ask God to forgive you for your sins and those who have sinned against you, this way you can come before God with a clean heart 3.) Praise God and thank him for who he is and what he has done in your life, thank him for watching over you and your family (you don't want to rush or get into the habit of always asking God for something when you pray, sometimes he just wants to hear "Thank You"). 4.) Make your request known to your father and cast all of your cares upon him, knowing that he cares for you.

Not sure if many have seen the movie "War Room" but I loved this movie because it showed the Power of Prayer and the authority that you have over the Devil when you constantly commune with God. The main Character, Elizabeth was battling constant attacks in her life until she met Miss Clara; she introduced Elizabeth to prayer and she immediately when home and cleared out her closet; which turned into her personal Prayer Closet. It is important to have a quiet place that you can go to God in prayer (a closet in your home, the bathroom, a room in your home, if you are at work you can go in your car on your lunch break, or find a quiet place). This is your private time with God to make your request known to him and to speak with him comfortably (Philippians 4:6). Anything that you want God to do concerning your life or manifest in your life you should do in prayer. James 4:2-3 tells us that we do not have a lot of things because we don't ask God for them; this passage also tells us that we must ask with the right motives in mind. I used to go to my car a lot at my previous duty station and have come out of my car feeling very refreshed and at peace. I have also had many encounters with God in my car. Prayer is and can be very refreshing, the Holy Spirit also gave me the gift of tongues right at home in my room after I read (Acts 2:1-13). Prayer is your personal relationship with God and can become a key tool in you dealing with everyday stress concerning your job, career, marriage, business and children. The Bible also tells us to pray without ceasing and not to pray and worry (1 Thessalonians 5: 16-18, Philippians 4:6-7). You also want to make sure that you are going to God in the name of Jesus, remember you have to go through God first in order to get to the son.

Prayer

Father God in the name of Jesus, we come before you with our hearts as pure as we know how. We thank you for getting us through this fast thus far. Lord, teach us how to pray strategic so that our prayers do not go in vain (Matthew 6:7). Teach us to develop a lifestyle of prayer so that we can communicate with you on a constant basis. Help us not to rush into Prayer asking you for things, but just to take some time out today to tell you how grateful and wonderful you are! We thank you Lord for forgiving us for all of our sins and dying on the cross for us; we don't know where we would be without you (Hebrews 9:28, John 15:13, 1 Corinthians 15: 3-4). In Jesus Name I pray, Amen!

Questions/Reflection

1. Each person is different, ask God to show you ways on how to increase your prayer closet or area.
2. Think of some quiet places that you can meet God at.

Day 11

The Halfway Mark

I can do all things through him who strengthens me.
(Philippians 4:13)

CONGRATULATIONS, YOU ARE HALFWAY There! Did you ever believe that you would make it this far on your fasting Journey? You should be very proud of yourself. Fasting has so many great benefits. I pretty sure by now you have lost weight, you are feeling much better, you have more energy, you are starting to feel the presence of God more, and you have more than likely lost a couple of pounds. I remember the first time I fasted for 21 days. It feel so good because not only was it life changing but, It helped me to be disciplined to turn down certain foods. There were also certain foods that I no longer wanted. When you fast, your taste buds will begin to change because you are detoxing your body of many toxins that were bad. I just want to encourage you at this point, don't give up and keep pressing towards the Mark (Philippians 3:14).

Prayer

Father God in the Name of Jesus, we just want to let you know today that we are grateful that you have brought us this far (1 Peter 5:10). We know that we would not have made it this far without you. Lord, we thank you for covering us daily with your Mercy and your Strength. Help us to continue to press on! We know that we can do this with your help. We thank you for your presence that surrounds us daily God; we thank you for the weight-loss and the health benefits that you have allowed us to experience through Prayer and Fasting. Lord, we ask that you move speedily on any situation within our lives and we thank you for honoring our sacrifice on today, in Jesus Name we pray, Amen!

Questions/Reflection

1. What are some great experiences that you have had with fasting this far?
2. Do you feel as though you can continue to fast? If Not, why?

Day 12

Discipleship

"Then said Jesus to those Jews which believed on him, If ye continue in my word, then are ye, my disciples, indeed; And ye shall know the truth, and the truth shall make you free."

John 8:31-32

DEFINITION OF A DISCIPLE—a follower, one who accepts and assist in spreading the doctrines of Jesus Christ

As a disciple and a leader of Jesus Christ, we must put all things concerning him first (Mark 8:34-38). As a leader of Christ, we must look different than everyone else and remember that we are living in the world but not of it (John 17:14-15). I believe that each person has a form of discipleship within them. Whether that's praying for others, telling someone about Jesus who doesn't know about him, assisting others on our Job and sharing our own testimonies about Jesus Christ so that others may see his glory. Discipleship also helps us to compare what the Holy Spirit prompts us to do with the Word of God. Sometimes the Holy Spirit will lead us into assignments that God has called us to do. For example, God gave me the assignment to write this book, along with "The Prayer and Fasting Kick-Start group on Facebook. Although I felt as though I was distracted along the way, The Holy Spirit continued to push me and lead me into completing my assignment. The Holy Spirit has also led me to pray with certain people in my workplace, especially if they came to me with personal issues in their lives. There were many times that I did not pray for that person and the Holy Spirit convicted me about it. Discipleship often means following the Holy Spirt and being obedient to Jesus Christ. There may also be times when you may feel as though you are walking with Christ alone; you may also feel like you are not a part of a certain group of people. No need to feel like this, sometimes being a true leader of Christ means standing alone. I am here today to let you know that whatever God is calling you to do; you have the authority, power, and strength to do it by the blood of Jesus Christ! Don't let anyone stray you away from your assignment, you don't need anyone's approval but God…So, go be great!

Prayer

Father God in the Name of Jesus, we come before you today as humbly as we know how. God, we thank you for giving us the power and authority through your son Jesus to complete the task that you have given us at hand. Lord, help us only to seek approval from you and not others. Lord, we ask for clarity about ways that we can save souls for your Kingdom. Lead us into the path of righteousness for your name sake. Help us not to be afraid to stand alone and stand out for Jesus. Teach us new ways to spread your word to your people, in any and every way possible. In Jesus Name we pray, Amen!

Questions/Reflection

1. What assignment do you feel like God has called you to do?
2. In what ways do you think you could lead people closer to Jesus?
3. How do you feel like you can assist others in getting to know Jesus Christ better?

Day 13

A Lifestyle of Fasting

"Therefore also now, saith the Lord, turn with all your heart, and with fasting, and with weeping, and with mourning."

Joel 2:12

I WILL NEVER FORGET the first time I fasted for 21 days. It was an experience that I will never forget. God revealed so many things to me, and I drew nearer to God like I never had before (James 4:8). As I began to seek God through prayer and Worship, I could feel my spirit separating from my flesh. I could also hear God's voice so much more clear. Words that my co-workers spoke at the time no longer became just words but, I stopped looking at things in the natural and began look at things in a spiritual sense. When you choose to fast not only does it build up your spiritual Man, but it also helps you begin to change your relationship with certain foods; it makes you more disciplined in that area. The first time I fasted I lost 12 lbs. and managed to keep it off for years. I also noticed that after my first fast, it became easier and easier to fast. For example: After I did the Daniels Fast for 21 day I was able to do Intermittent fasting for longer periods of time, (which I never thought I would be able to commit to) I was also able to fast for a full day without food. Keep in mind though; God had to lead me to do this, as I recognize I would not be able to do it on my own. Fasting will definitely help you lose weight and put you back in control of your temptations. It will also help you to find out God's will for your life and which path God's wants you to take.

Prayer

I Pray in Jesus Name that not only does your prayer life increase through fasting but that you will begin to seek God like never before. I pray that God decreases your fleshly desires and builds up your Spirit Man. I pray that God changes your circle of friends and begins to place people in your life that have a purpose. Anyone that is not meant to be where God is trying to take you, I pray that you are released from them today in Jesus Name. I pray that this Fast helps you not only to hear more clearly from God but that it changes your relationship with Food. I decree and declare that from this day forward you will never be the same. In Jesus Name I pray Amen!

Questions/Reflection

1. Why did you choose to fast?
2. Are you beginning to hear more clearly from God since you have been fasting?
3. What do you plan to gain from partaking in Fasting?

Day 14

Health & Wellness

"So whatever you eat or drink or whatever you do, do it all for the glory of God."

1 Corinthians 10:31

BIBLICALLY SPEAKING, WHAT DOES Health & Wellness truly mean? You hear many people talk about this, but do we know what it feels like to truly experience Health and Wellness through the grace of God? I would like to discuss some scriptures on what God's idea of true health and wellness is. The bible tells us that whatever we eat or drink, to do it to the Glory of God (1 Corinthians 10:31). My interpretation is that we should be mindful of what we allow our bodies to consume. For example, it's ok to enjoy sweet treats (cakes, cookies & candies) every now and then, but we definitely don't want to over indulge to the point to where we become overweight. What we drink is very important also because we must remind ourselves that we are to do this unto God's liking. If we are consuming a lot of drinks that may cause our bodies a lot of harm in the long run (excessive alcohol, sugary energy drinks, sodas), then we technically are not glorifying God. It is ok to have these things now and then, but we are also reminded that we were bought with a price (1

Corinthians 6:20) and that we should take care of our temples. Stress has a lot to do with Health and Wellness also. Although, we may not realize it, if there are many issues and problems weighing us down in our lives this can also affect our health. For example, Psalm 38: 3-8 tells us that our anger and stress can lead to us being overwhelmed, unhealthy and exhausted. I want to encourage you today to cast your cares upon the Lord (Matthew 11:28-29) and don't allow anything to stress you out because it could very well cost you your life. I also encourage you to fill your spirit with the word of God every day. Don't allow negative people or energy to overtake you. (Proverbs 17:22, Isaiah 58:11). Worry about nothing, pray about everything!

Prayer

Dear Lord, we come before you today to thank you for leading and guiding us into true Health and Wellness through your son Jesus Christ. Lord, help us to cast all of our cares upon you today so that we can live a stress-free life. Lord, we also ask that you show us on today anything that may be causing our bodies' long-term stress or illness. Help us to remember that our bodies are supposed to be used to glorify you and that by serving you and doing your will, you will protect us from illness (Exodus 23:25). We Speak life over our bodies today, in Jesus Name Amen!

Questions/Reflection

1. Is there anything weighing you down today that you need to give to God?
2. What are some things that you can change in your life today to experience true Health and Wellness?

Day 15

The Detoxing Process

"Create in me a clean heart, O God, and renew a right spirit within me."

Psalm 51:10

WHEN IT COMES TO detoxing, sometimes the process can get very ugly. Why? Because it doesn't feel good, not only must we detox our bodies, but we must also detox our mind and soul (spirit). I truly believe that this will start us on the road to true deliverance. To do this, there is a process that God must take us through. For example, the first time I detoxed, my natural fleshly body went through a hard time. I experienced stomach pains, nausea, and headaches. You ask why? Because I was in taking caffeine, sweets, and sugar before my fast. When my flesh started to go without these things, I went through a process of feeling tired and groggy for a couple of days. This was because my body was ridding me of toxins. I also believe that we must detox our minds. This includes a process of changing the way we think or in other words, "renewing our minds." Romans 12:2 tells us that we are to be transformed by the renewing of our minds so that we can test and approve what God's will is. To be truly transformed we must detox our minds. This could be a long process, but this is also why it is important to guard our hearts and minds when fasting (Proverbs 4:23). For example, this is why I would suggest fasting from certain television shows, certain things watched on the internet, YouTube, Facebook, Instagram, Snap Chat, etc. As we all know (for those a part of the social media world), there are certain things that are shared on pages that we have no control over. These things could be homosexuality, sexual or violent. Think of your mind as a computer, what you feed your brain is very important. For example: if God has just recently delivered you from fornication or homosexuality. There may be certain TV shows that you might not want to watch anymore because it may stir up some old spirits that you don't want to enter back into your life.

Prayer

Lord Jesus, I thank you for renewing my spirit and cleansing my heart. Lord I also ask that you help me to refrain from watching things on television or social media that are not pleasing to you. Allow me to push those things to the side and to stay totally focused on you and your word during this fast. I thank you for a renewed mind, body and soul on today! I am being made over and I love you for that. Thank you for loving me, in Jesus name I pray Amen.

Questions/Reflection

1. What are some things you feel that you need to detox from?
2. What are you having a hard time with?

Day 16

Spiritual Gifts (The Holy Spirit)

1 Corinthians 12:1-11

ONCE THE HOLY SPIRIT is received, there are nine gifts that the Holy Spirit can give you. These Nine gifts are Knowledge, Wisdom, Prophecy, Faith, Healings, Miracles, Discerning of Spirits, and Different Types of Tongues & Interpretation of Tongues. I believe that if you go to our Lord in Prayer and ask him for these gifts, he will release them unto you in due time. The gift of Knowledge & Wisdom comes from knowing the Word of God and studying it (1 Corinthians 12:8). Once you began to have a relationship with God, he will release his secrets to you (Isaiah 45:3). The Gift of Prophecy is someone (women or man) that God has appointed to speak through. Some famous prophets in the bible were Amos, Ezekiel, Daniel, Jeremiah, Isaiah, Hosea, Jonah, Zephaniah, and Haggai & Zechariah. Some of you may have had an encounter with a prophet or prophetess, and they have prophesied something to you that came to pass. You also have to be careful though because the bible tells us to be aware of false prophets (Matthew 7: 15-20).

God may put it in your spirit to speak a word to someone who may be feeling down, or you may be able to see things in the spirit about certain people, this may mean that you have a gift of prophecy. Faith is also another gift; most people may not realize it because of situations and events in their lives. The Bible tells us that faith can move mountains (Matthew 17:20). Faith can take you a long way, imagine yourself praying for a sick family member that may have possibly been declared dead and God brought that family member back to life right in front of you. Another example of faith is stepping out and starting a business or applying for a home loan when in actuality you have no idea where the money will come from. The reason that faith is a gift is because everyone doesn't have it. For example, if you always hear people speak negatively over their situation (or yours), or hear comments like: I am always stressed, I can't win, this will never work. These are words of defeat. No need to get upset, this is an example of an individual that has no faith. Another Gift of the Spirit is Healing, Where God has given you the gift to lay your hands on an individual, and they be healed. Remember in the bible the women with the issue of blood? (Luke 8: 43-48). She touched Jesus' garment and was immediately healed. Ask Jesus to give you the gift of healing today. Another Gift is the gift of Miracles, as you already know or may have heard, Jesus performed many miracles in the bible including allowing Lazarus to get up and walk after being dead for four days. If you look at John 11:14-15, Jesus waited after Lazarus's sisters had sent for him. Lazarus was already dead when Jesus brought him back to life (John 11:43-44). But, he did this purposely so that the glory of God would be revealed. You may also have heard the famous story about Jesus feeding 5000 people (read John 6:1-15). This is when Jesus took two fish, five barley loaves & fed thousands of people. Jesus performed a Miracle. We have to remember that we also have this same authority (Luke 10:19). The Discerning of Spirits (which is one of the gifts the Holy Spirit gave me) is when the Holy Spirit gives you the ability to detect things that may not be right in the atmosphere. A lot of times this gives you the ability to detect different kinds of spirts (good or bad) in people. Have you ever been around someone and you sense an evil presence? Or, have you ever visited a certain church, and you just don't feel like the presence of God is there? This is called discernment my friend, and you may very well have this gift. Different Types of tongues and interpretations of tongues is another Spiritual Gift that the Holy Spirit has given me. I love this gift and believe that it is very special because it allows you to speak in a language that only you and God understand. The bible tells us that when we speak in an unknown tongue, we speak mysteries unto heaven (1 Corinthians 14:2). The bible also tells us that the gift of tongues does many things: it increases your prayer life, it edifies you, and it gives you revelation on many things. An example of The gift to interpret tongues is when God will anoint someone to interpret the language of tongues that are spoken. Although the bible talks about speaking in tongues in the church, it also lets us know that if done in the church, there should be someone there to interpret (1 Corinthians 14:27).

Prayer

Father God in the Name of Jesus, we come before you right now to thank you for the gifts of the Holy Spirit (The word of knowledge, wisdom, prophecy, faith, healing, miracles, discernment, tongues and the interpretation of tongues). Thank you holy spirit for creating these gifts for your people. I pray that you allow me to receive them today (whether it's meant for me to have one, or all). Move by your spirit Lord, I receive these spiritual gifts today, in Jesus Name I pray Amen.

Questions/Reflection

1. What Spiritual Gifts have you received? (If you haven't received any Spiritual Gifts yet, are you prepared to ask God for them today?).
2. Spiritual Gifts are a blessing, Set out some time today, get in God's presence and ask him for these gifts (if you desire them). After all, you are a child of God and you are entitled to them.

Day 17

Generational Curses

"You shall not bow down to them or serve them, for I the Lord your God am a jealous God, visiting the iniquity of the fathers on the children to the third and the fourth generation of those who hate me."

Exodus 20:5

GENERATIONAL CURSES ARE VERY real; a lot of the spirits and traits that we have were carried on through generations. For example, you may recognize that some of the same things you struggle with today, your great grandparents and grandparents have struggled with also. Some of these same traits (good or bad) can be carried onto our children and grandchildren. This is why it is very important for Mothers to speak life and pray over their children while they are in our womb. There are many generational spirits and traits that God has revealed to me within my own family. For example: I noticed the Spirit of Addiction with Alcoholism in my Uncle and Father. I also at one point in my life struggled with Alcohol. I would wake up in the morning and drink five beers before 10:00 am. I also noticed myself drinking heavily on the Weekend. I would buy liquor on Friday evening, and the whole bottle would be gone my Sunday evening. This was something I had picked up on my own, but at the same time it wasn't a coincidence that my Father struggled with this very ugly demon as well. I will admit that I do drink wine now and then, but the word of God tells us not to get drunk (Ephesians 5:18). Which was very well what I was doing. I also noticed that my Mother struggled badly with finances growing up (this included paying bills on time, checks bouncing & misspending). To be totally transparent with you, I did and still struggle with some of these same traits today. Although the Holy Spirit is helping me to get back on track, the bible tells us to be good stewards over our finances (Proverbs 13:11). Ask God to reveal any and every generational curse that your family may be struggling with Today. I decree and declare this day that God will use you to break the cycle of addiction & poverty within your generation. Remember you are different, you don't have to do what your grandparents or parents did. Break free and be you today!

Prayer

Father God in the Name of Jesus, I come before you today asking that you cover me from any and every demonic assignment or attack that Satan and his Kingdom have tried to implant within my family today. Satan, I come against you and your fallen angels with any generational curses that are trying to overtake my children and I. In the Name of Jesus, I rebuke all cycles of bad habits including drugs, alcohol, poverty, bad financial decisions, gossiping, gambling, fornication, spirts of molestation, lust, perversion, spirits of masturbation, incest, etc. I decree and declare today that you will use me, Father to come out from amongst them (2 Corinthians 6:17) and break these cycles. Father, help to realize that I am different and you will use me to save my family from the pits of hell. Satan I send you, your demonic angels and your entire Kingdom back to the pits of hell from which you came! Lastly, Father God, I ask that you post a hedge of protection around myself, my family, my children, my grandchildren and their children and many generations that will come after me. Father, I thank you in advance for making me a legend, which will greatly be remembered. In Jesus Mighty Name I pray, Amen!

Questions/Reflection

1. Ask God to show you Generational Curses that may be lingering within your family?
2. Are there any generational traits that your grandparents struggled with that you see yourself struggling with today?
3. Speak This Declaration over Generational Curses concerning your family
4. I plead the blood of Jesus and rebuke any and every lingering Generational Curse over my forefathers, My great grandparents, grandparents, myself and my children Today in Jesus Name!

Day 18

Faith

"Now faith is the substance of things hoped for, the evidence of things not seen."

Hebrews 11:1

THE DEFINITION OF FAITH is complete trust or confidence in someone or something (God/Jesus Christ). What does it truly mean to operate in faith? Imagined how awesome our lives would be if we truly lived by faith. Imagine going to look for a house that we haven't gotten approved for yet, applying for that job (when most people would say you are under qualifying) or jumping out there to start a business when most people may tell you that you are crazy and that it won't work out. Imagined if we stopped listening to what man said and started listening to what God said about us. When I first started my fitness/ spiritual health and wellness ministry I had a lot of people (even within my own family) tell me that it was a bad idea. That I should use my Computer Science degree and that I wouldn't get a lot of clientele being a personal trainer. But, the Holy Spirit that lives within me had me to keep striving. Just to tell you some of my testimony, I was on military active duty orders for two years and I absolutely hated it. I mean, the money was good but the environment and people that I worked with were very harsh. I found myself fasting, praying and crying out to God about my purpose. I knew that this wasn't how my life was supposed to go. I knew God had something else for me. I began to pray for God to take me off of my Job (which he did in July 2016). For a year, I became a stay at home mom (with the help of my husband's support). I began to focus on God, my husband and my children. This is when I also began to focus on Crystalline Solid LLC. (My fitness business). For the rest of 2016 and 2017, God began to reveal my purpose to me slowly. God also led me to write this book. I began to have a passion to not only help people get into shape, but to lead the people of God into a lifestyle of prayer and fasting. I began to enjoy what I wanted to do and told God that I no longer wanted to work in "Corporate America". Although at first, the money for the business was slow, I was determined to make it work. I began to work the works that God gave me (John 9:4). God helped me to exercise my faith and I slowly no longer started to care what other people's opinion of me was. I knew that God was on my side and that he would never give me a vision without a plan (Proverbs 16: 3, 9). I also began to keep a lot of things to myself, as I quietly showed up and showed out in the fitness industry. I am here to encourage you to step out on faith with whatever God has told you to do. You don't need anyone's approval. Don't be fearful (Isaiah 41:10). Walk into your purpose and what God has for you.

Questions/Reflection

1. Habakkuk 2:3-3 says to write the vison down and make it plain. I encourage you to write down every vison that God has given you and pray over it! I promise you that your vision will come to pass at an appointed time.

Prayer

Father God, in the Name of Jesus we ask you for the strength to walk out on faith today. Lord, help us to write our vision down to you and make it plain so that you may allow us to carry it out. Deliver us from other people's opinions and what they may have said about our lives. Lord help us to walk out in faith concerning whatever it is that we are hoping for (a new house, a new career path, a new job, a renewed mind or a new business). Help us to put works towards our faith (John 9:4), knowing that there is work that we must do, in order to see results. That work could be paying off debts to see a higher credit scores, putting in job applications, updating resumes, renewing our mind daily with the Word of God or saving up money slowly to start our business. Lord, we know that with you on our side, anything is possible (Luke 1:37). In Jesus Name I pray, Amen!

Questions/Reflection

1. Are you willing to take the first step out on faith today concerning the things that you want God to do in your life?
2. What are you hoping for God to do concerning your (career, business, spouse or children)?

Day 19

The Anointing

"As for you, the anointing you received from him remains in you, and you do not need anyone to teach you. But as his anointing teaches you about all things and as that anointing is real, not counterfeit-just as it has taught you, remain in him."

1 John 2:27

BEING ANOINTING IS SIMPLY being effective, not to be confused with style or swagger. For example, honestly speaking I feel as though a lot of pastors, apostles, teachers, and prophets take each other's methods, and don't have a real anointing because they are trying to mock someone else. When I visit different churches, I notice a lot of Pastors may speak very loudly or grunt when they preach. I am very quiet and meek because that is how God created me. Therefore the way I pray is very different than the way others may Pray. There is no need to feel intimidated by the way another individual may Worship or Pray. All you need to know is that every anointing is going to cost you something. For example: To become more effective in Prayer you may need to get up earlier in the morning, or spend more time in prayer (this also can increase by spending more time in God's word). To become more effective in Worship, you may have to increase your worship time from 5 min to 15 min, then once you Master that 15 min, increase to 30 min. To become more effective in speaking in tongues, you may have to increase the number of times you speak in tongues per day. Does this make sense? We as the People of God have to learn not to compare our lifestyles with others because we don't know what they went through to get that anointing. The Power of God is what makes you effective. When you are anointed, you don't have to worry about being like anyone else because everyone's anointing is different. God will make you useful in your very own way. Believe me, When God (not man) anoints you, you will know.

Prayer

Father God, our Savior, we come before you right now to thank you for the anointing that you have placed upon my life, whatever it may be God, we ask that you make it effective Today. Lord, help us to accept who we are in you. Help us not to feel the need to copy or take anyone else's prayer lifestyle, preaching, teaching, or prophetic lifestyles. Lord we thank you for creating us differently, In Jesus Name we pray, Amen!

Questions/Reflection

1. Ask God to anoint you through his Power.
2. In What ways do you feel like God will or has made you effective thus far?

Day 20

Favor

"In him, we have obtained an inheritance, having been predestined according to the purpose of him who works all things according to the counsel of his will."

(Ephesians 1:11)

DO YOU REALIZE THAT God has predestined your future? Every good thing that has and is happening to you is supposed to happen, What do I mean? Because God loves you, he is going to make every situation in your life possible according to his will and purpose for your life. One of the many definitions of favor is, "an act of kindness that is beyond what is due or unusual. In the eyes of someone else that may look upon your life and see the way that God blesses you, they may say that "favor isn't fair." Well, they are right, favor isn't fair. God has favor upon us not necessarily because we deserve it, but because he is good and we have earned approval in his eyes. God's view towards us is the only view that should matter. We should not look for approval toward our family or friends but only towards God. You will be shocked (if you haven't become shocked already) because God will begin to pour blessings upon you. You may feel as though you don't deserve it, but you do! Don't worry about what others say about you. People will wonder why God has blessed you with that house, that car or how you got approved for that business loan. Well, guess what, let them wonder because it's all a part of God's plan for your life. You haven't seen anything yet! The best is yet to come.

Prayer

Father God in Jesus Name, I thank you for blessing me with so many things in my life. I know I may not deserve these things but you have given them to me because you a good and merciful God. Lord God, you know the plans you have for my future! I thank you for being all seeing and all knowing. I appreciate the fact that you love me so much. I anticipate the blessings that you will pour upon my family and I for many years to come. Thank you, God, for favor, in Jesus name Amen.

Questions/Reflection

1. Have you ever looked at someone else's life and wondered, "How did they receive that?" If so why?
2. In what ways have you felt that you have obtained favor from God thus far?

Day 21

Breakthrough

And ye shall know the truth, and the truth shall make you free.

John 8:32

THE DEFINITION OF BREAKTHROUGH is a sudden or dramatic discovery or development; a leap forward.

You may ask yourself? What is a breakthrough? A breakthrough is precisely what it sounds like. Imagine yourself "breaking through something." You have come to the last day of your fast, and I am here to decree and declare to you that whatever you have been asking God to do in your life for the past 21 days just know that it is about to happen. God is about to put you at the head of the line (Matthew 20:16). You are about to shoot past family members that may be more educated than you. Many of you are going to receive promotions on a job and you have only been there for a couple of months (verses someone who may have been there for years). You have sacrificed something, you have pushed your plate aside, and you have become stronger in your walk with God. Believe me when I say God is going to bless you. Get ready, get prepared because God is going to move very quickly on your behalf. Many believers may know you were fasting because sometimes spirits can recognize familiar spirits. Since you have been fasting, God's glory is shining all upon you! Some of you have never fasted before, and God is paying attention now, he heard your cry, and he is going to answer every question that you have. If you feel as though you haven't heard from God yet, don't worry, he may very well be testing you. Remember, God does things on his time and he is still going to operate in your life not just after these 21 days, but for many years to come. Hold on to God's unchanging hand and continue to stand on his word and be encouraged… this is just the beginning!

Prayer

Father God in the Name of Jesus, I thank you that my breakthrough is just right around the corner. I thank you, God, for allowing me to complete 21 days of prayer and fasting. I understand God that this wasn't for you, but for me. I have learned so much from this fast, and I give you all honor and glory for that. I receive my breakthrough right now! In Jesus Name Amen.

Questions/Reflections:

1. What have you gained spiritually, physically and mentally from fasting in 21 days?
2. Do you have more of a desire to fast now that you ever had before?
3. Have you experienced a breakthrough yet? If so, share you testimony with someone. If not, remember God's timing is the best and believe me; he has something great prepared for you!

About the Author

CRYSTAL NICOLE WILSON IS an online fitness trainer and a Spiritual Health and Wellness counselor. She is the founder of Crystalline Solid LLC, (an inspirational and motivational online fitness community for men and women). Crystal is a member of the United States Armed Forces and is also a graduate from Limestone College (Bachelor of Science degree). She shares her only personal testimony with fasting, how she struggled with it and what blessings she received from it. Crystal includes scripture through this devotional (not only taking you through the spiritual aspect of it but the physical and mental). Crystal wants to be a servant of God, be real with people of God and reach those who may not know Jesus. She prays that many souls are saved from reading this book and that the kingdom of God will be redeemed.

www.ingramcontent.com/pod-product-compliance
Lightning Source LLC
LaVergne TN
LVHW011210080426
835508LV00007B/705